W9-BZE-439

FOCUS ON
FAMILY
MATTERS

Dealing with
the Loss of
a Loved One

FOCUS ON FAMILY MATTERS

Focus on Family Matters

Dealing with the Loss of a Loved One

Sara L. Latta

Marvin Rosen, Ph.D.
Consulting Editor

CHELSEA HOUSE
P U B L I S H E R S
A Haights Cross Communications Company
Philadelphia

CHELSEA HOUSE PUBLISHERS

EDITOR IN CHIEF Sally Cheney
DIRECTOR OF PRODUCTION Kim Shinners
CREATIVE MANAGER Takeshi Takahashi
MANUFACTURING MANAGER Diann Grasse

Staff for DEALING WITH THE LOSS OF A LOVED ONE

ASSOCIATE EDITOR Bill Conn
PICTURE RESEARCHER Sarah Bloom
PRODUCTION ASSISTANT Jaimie Winkler
SERIES DESIGNER Takeshi Takahashi
LAYOUT 21st Century Publishing and Communications, Inc.

A Haights Cross Communications ✦ Company

http://www.chelseahouse.com

First Printing

1 3 5 7 9 8 6 4 2

Library of Congress Cataloging-in-Publication Data

Latta, Sara L.
    Dealing with the loss of a loved one : focus on family matters / Sara Latta.
        p. cm.
Includes bibliographical references and index.
    ISBN 0-7910-6955-9
    1. Grief in adolescence—Juvenile literature. 2. Bereavement in adolescence—Juvenile
literature. 3. Loss (Psychology) in adolescence—Juvenile literature. 4. Teenagers and
death—Juvenile literature. [1. Grief. 2. Death.] I. Title.
BF724.3.G73 L38 2002
155.9'37—dc21

*The advice and suggestions given in this book are not meant to replace professional
medical or psychiatric care. Readers are advised to seek professional help if they
suspect that they are suffering from clinical depression or another mental illness. The
author disclaims liability for any loss or risk, personal or otherwise, resulting directly
or indirectly from the use, application, or interpretation of the contents of this book.*

Contents

Introduction

Marvin Rosen, Ph.D.
Consulting Editor

B ad things sometimes happen to good people. We've probably all heard that expression. But what happens when the "good people" are teenagers?

Growing up is stressful and difficult to negotiate. Teenagers are struggling to becoming independent, trying to cut ties with their families that they see as restrictive, burdensome, and unfair. Rather than attempting to connect in new ways with their parents, they may withdraw. When bad things do happen, this separation may make the teen feel alone in coping with difficult and stressful issues.

Focus on Family Matters provides teens with practical information about how to cope when bad things happen to them. The series deals foremost with feelings—the emotional pain associated with adversity. Grieving, fear, anger, stress, guilt, and sadness are addressed head on. Teens will gain valuable insight and advice about dealing with their feelings, and for seeking help when they cannot help themselves.

The authors in this series identify some of the more serious problems teens face. In so doing, they make three assumptions: First, teens who find themselves in difficult situations are not at fault and should not blame themselves. Second, teens can overcome difficult situations, but may need help to do so. Third, teens bond with their families, and the strength of this bond influences their ability to handle difficult situations.

These books are also about communication—specifically about the value of communication. None of the problems covered occurs in a vacuum, and none of the situations should be faced by anyone alone. Each either involves a close family member or affects the entire family. Since families teach teens how to trust, relate to others, and solve problems, teens need to bond with families to develop normally and become emotionally whole. Success in dealing with adversity depends not only on the strength of the individual teen, but also upon the resources of the family in providing support, advice, and material assistance. Strong attachment to care givers in a supporting, nurturing, safe family structure is essential to successful coping.

Some teens learn to cope with adversity—they absorb the pain, they adjust, and they go on. But for others, the trauma they experience seems like an insurmountable challenge—they become angry, stressed, and depressed. They may withdraw from friends, they may stop going to school, and their grades may slip. They may draw negative attention to themselves and express their pain and fear by rebelling. Yet, in each case, healing can occur.

The teens who cope well with adversity, who are able to put the past behind them and regain their momentum, are no less sensitive or caring than those who suffer most. Yet there is a difference. Teens who are more resilient to trauma are able to dig deep down into their own resources, to find strength in their families and in their own skills, accomplishments, goals, aspirations, and values. They are able to find reasons for optimism and to feel confidence in their capabilities. This series recognizes the effectiveness of these strategies, and presents problem-solving skills that every teen can use.

Focus on Family Matters is positive, optimistic, and supportive. It gives teens hope and reinforces the power of their own efforts to handle adversity. And most importantly, it shows teens that while they cannot undo the bad things that have happen, they have the power to shape their own futures and flourish as healthy, productive adults.

When Someone You Love Has Died

■ Jen's world fell apart one cool autumn evening with a simple telephone call. She watched as her mother answered the phone, turned pale, and sank into a chair. Her older brother, Jason, had been killed in a car accident. Jen's family later learned that Jason and his friends, including the driver of the car, had all been drinking before the accident. Brad, the driver, walked away with minor injuries; Jason and two other friends were killed instantly. Jen wondered if she could have done something to prevent Jason's death. After all, she'd known that he and his friends drank occasionally. If only she'd told her parents . . .

At Jason's funeral, it seemed that everyone was crying but Jen. She just felt numb. Jen half-expected her brother to come sauntering into the church with his trademark devil-may-care look on his face. In the days after the funeral, Jen's mother spent countless hours in Jason's room: dusting his dresser, rearranging his soccer trophies, handling his pet lizards. She seemed to forget that she had a living daughter! Jen's dad prayed a lot. Jen couldn't understand praying to a God who would take her brother away. Brad and his parents came to their house to apologize for his actions and ask for their forgiveness. Jen watched, arms crossed, as her mother embraced Brad and her father solemnly shook his hand. Jen wanted to smash a vase over his head

Things were not much better at school. She couldn't concentrate, and often forgot her homework assignments. Kids she had known since kindergarten hurried by her as the passed in the hall. Jen's best friend said, "I know just how you feel. When my grandma died, I thought I'd never get over it." Jen wanted to slap her. Instead she yelled, "You have no idea how I feel!" and stormed away. She wondered if she were going crazy.

Someone you love has died, and nothing has prepared you for this terrible loss. If some of Jen's feelings seem familiar to you, you should know that you are not a alone. You are on the long, difficult journey called grieving, and you are normal. Perhaps someone you care about has lost a loved one, and you just can't find the right words to comfort your friend. This is normal, too. It's difficult to talk about death and dying, even though we hear about it nearly every day.

You've probably watched people die on television and at the movies—but you know that those deaths aren't real. You may have heard about a volcano in the Congo that killed dozens of people and felt sorry for the victims—but they're so far away. Or you read about students who went on a killing spree in their

How would you feel

if someone caused the death of a person you love? Could you forgive them?

Nothing can prepare you for the sudden death of a loved one. The feelings associated with grief are powerful and often overwhelming, but they are a normal reaction to loss.

high school, and thought, "Thank goodness that would never happen here." Yet death eventually touches us all.

Over two million people in the United States die each year. A baby dies every fifteen minutes. Forty thousand people from 10 to 24 years of age die each year; three quarters of those deaths are due to suicide, homicide, or car accidents. An adult with cancer dies every minute. In one recent survey, 87% of teens indicated that they knew another teenager who had died.

It can be hard to accept the fact that someone close to you has died. A younger brother or sister may believe that Grandma will eventually wake up, but you are old enough to understand that death is final. But it will take some time for your heart to truly feel that your loved one is gone. Like Jen, you may imagine that he or she will come back into your life, saying, "It was all a big mistake. That wasn't me you buried—it was someone else!" Talking about what has happened with people you trust will not only help you, but will help your friends and family accept the reality of your loved one's death as well. Many teens find that keeping a journal is wonderful therapy.

If you are close to someone who recently lost a loved one, you may wonder at first whether you should say something. You may think that your friend doesn't want to be reminded of the loss. But in the beginning, you friend can probably think of little else. A simple "I'm sorry to hear about your brother. He was a great guy" helps your friend—and you—to accept the reality of death.

> **What would you say**
>
> **to make a friend feel better after someone close to them has died?**

Losing a loved one can stir up all sorts of scary emotions—sadness, of course, but also anger, guilt, fear, regret. **Grief** can be all of these emotions and more—it can also appear in the form of headaches, inability to sleep or eat, or forgetfulness, to name a few. In the following chapters, we'll explore the different faces of grief, and discuss ways of coping. You will learn about

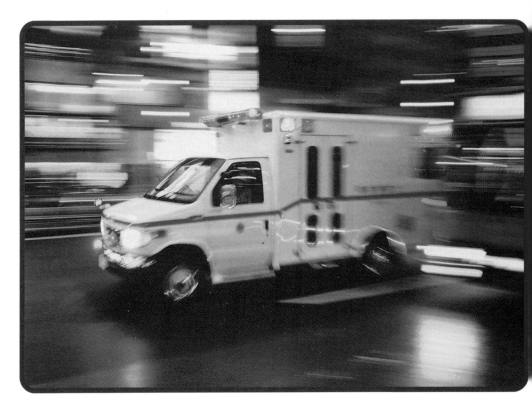

It is a sad statistic that three of four deaths among people 10 to 24 years of age are the result of suicide, murder, or car accidents. Accepting a painful loss takes time, and it is important to be patient with yourself and those around you who are grieving.

the ways we say goodbye, though funerals, memorial services, and other **rituals**. We will talk about the ways your family and social life might change after someone you love has died. We will discuss some special circumstances, including dealing with death resulting from suicide or disasters. Finally, you'll learn about what you can do to get on with your life, even as you find meaningful ways to remember your loved one throughout the days and years to come.

Growing up is hard work. You are learning to become more independent from you parents, even as you continue to depend on them for many things. You are figuring out who you are, and what your place is in the world. Grieving is hard work, too. You must come to terms with the fact that you will never see your loved one again and allow yourself to express your grief. Your world has changed; part of grieving is finding ways to adjust to life without your loved one. You'll find a way to finally say goodbye to your loved one and move on with your life. Grieving while you're growing up may seem to be more than you can bear. But remember that while losing someone you love will change you, it need not destroy you. You will survive.

What would you do

to help yourself adjust to a new life after the death of someone you love?

Grieving for a Loved One

James had always been close to Pop—the name he had called his grandfather since he was a little boy. Pop lived with James and his mother, who worked the evening shift at the hospital. He was always there to take care of James after school and at night. During baseball season, James and Pop went to White Sox games every weekend they played at home.

When James was fourteen years old, he came home from school one day to find Pop lying on the kitchen floor. James knelt to check his grandfather's pulse, only to find that Pop's body felt cool and stiff. Doctors told James and his mother that Pop had died of a heart attack. Although James felt as though his own heart had been torn from his chest, he tried to act strong. He did not want his mother to worry.

The house was too quiet without Pop. Things that used to be easy for James now seemed impossibly hard: he completely forgot his lines when auditioning for the school play. Embarrassed, he stopped going to drama club. He dropped easy

Grief can leave us feeling alone, frightened, angry, or confused. Expressing our feelings with those close to us can help us move through the grief.

pop flies playing baseball with his friends, and made up excuses for why he couldn't play with them anymore.

One day, James came home to find two tickets to the first White Sox home game of the season lying on the kitchen table. "I want to take you," his mom told him, even though she had never sat through an entire baseball game in her life. At first, it didn't seem right to enjoy the game without Pop, but he found himself jumping up and down along with the rest of the crowd when the Sox scored their first run. When they returned to their apartment after the game, James hugged his mother and cried—the first time since Pop died. It felt surprisingly good.

When the wife of author C.S. Lewis died, he wrote, "No one ever told me that grief felt so like fear." You may also be discovering that grief can have many faces—not all of them what we imagined they might be. Your grief is your own, but it may help you to know that many people share some common reactions after a loved one has died.

How You May Feel

Have you ever accidentally hit your thumb hard with a hammer? At first, it doesn't hurt that much. The pain comes later. This is our body's way of protecting us from danger. Many people also feel numb just after they learn that someone they love has died—especially if the death was sudden or violent. Sometimes, teens try not to allow themselves to feel too much or cry because they are embarrassed or they want to protect others from their painful emotions. But crying and finding other ways of expressing our powerful emotions make us stronger. Think of tears as washing away the grief you're carrying inside.

What would you do to relieve some of the sadness associated with your grief?

When someone dear to you dies, you may feel as though you have been abandoned. No one can replace your loved one, but it is important to remember that there are others who care about you. Try reaching out to them; cultivate new friendships. If you fear that you will lose other friends or members of your family, make a practice of checking in with them as often as you can; just hearing their voices can be very reassuring.

It's very common to feel angry when someone you love has died. You might feel angry with the person who died: your friend drove recklessly and was killed in a car

Reaching out to others around you can help you cope with feelings of grief and anger after a loss. Remember that you are not alone—people care about you and want to help.

crash; your grandfather smoked and was overweight; your sister had unprotected sex and became infected with HIV. You lash out at your family because you have additional responsibilities, or at your friends when they make unthinking comments about your loss. You may be angry with God for allowing this horrible thing to happen.

It's okay to be angry, but you need to find ways to express your anger that won't hurt you or others. If you're angry with someone, try writing that person a long letter explaining how you feel and why. But don't mail it; tear it up, burn it—destroy it somehow. Try going for a run, riding your bike, shooting hoops—any physical activity that you enjoy. Hit a punching bag or whack a pillow with a tennis racket. Talk to someone you trust. It's important to let your feelings out—bottled-up anger can hurt you and others around you.

Can you describe the activities and hobbies that may help you deal with your anger in a positive way?

You may be surprised to find that you feel relieved when your loved one has died—and then feel guilty for feeling that way! But if your loved one suffered before dying, or if it seemed that constant visits to the hospital made it impossible for you to lead a normal teenager's life, of course those feelings are normal. Perhaps the person who died abused you, or you argued a lot. You may have said—or thought—"I wish you were dead!" Now you feel guilty. But remember that we all say and do things that we shouldn't. Learn to forgive yourself.

When someone you love has died, it's normal to feel depressed—you feel as though you can't bear the pain, that nothing seems to matter any more. All you want to do is curl up on your bed and cry. You might feel exhausted even though you sleep a lot. **Depression** is normal after someone you love has died, often lasting a few days or weeks. But if you continue to feel this way after a couple of weeks, you may be heading toward clinical depression. It this is the case, or if you *ever* have thoughts of ending your own life, you should seek help with a mental health professional immediately. Clinical depression can be a serious problem; one that you may need help to overcome.

Is This Really My Body?

Grief can be hard on your body. Scientists have shown that **stress** can lower your immune defenses; you may find yourself picking up every passing cold virus. But stress can affect your body in other ways, too. You may feel that you are suddenly clumsy and uncoordinated. Your throat tightens up, making it difficult to breathe. Your heart pounds, your hands become cold and clammy, or you develop frequent headaches. Perhaps you grind your teeth at night, or develop embarrassing nervous twitches. Girls may experience changes in their menstrual cycle. You might find that your allergies or asthma are more difficult to control. All of these changes can be frightening—what if this means you're dying, too?

While physical changes are a normal part of grieving, it's important to recognize that your symptoms are real. It is a good idea to make an appointment with your family doctor, and to make sure that he or she knows that someone you love recently died. Your doctor can help you manage your symptoms.

Sometimes, physical symptoms arise because we do not allow ourselves to express powerful emotions. If you keep your anger bottled up inside, it may very well find

Grief can be stressful on you physically. You may experience a loss of appetite, problems sleeping, headaches, or other symptoms. Your family doctor may be able to help you cope with these common side-effects of grief.

its way out through stomach pains. You might not even realize that you are anxious and fearful, but these unacknowledged feelings might be responsible for your mysterious rash. If you are able to understand and

How can grief

create changes in your body? Can it make you physically sick?

express your feelings in positive ways, you may find that your physical symptoms disappear.

I Can't Think Straight!

Many people find that their brains just don't work very well after someone they love has died. Your mind will wander even in your favorite class, or you will be unable to complete a sentence because you can't remember what you were going to say. You forget to feed the cat, even though you've been doing it faithfully without being reminded for five years. You find yourself losing everything—your house keys, your math assignment, your sense of direction. Are you losing your mind, too?

No, it's just another face of grief. Think of it this way: your world has changed, and your brain is busy adapting, too. When you adjust to life without your loved one, your powers of concentration and memory will improve. Until then, there are some things you can do to help you manage your days.

If you have a hard time concentrating, you're probably having a hard time at school. Talk to your teachers so that they will be aware that you are going through a very difficult time. They may be willing to forgive late homework, or suggest ways of earning extra credit. You may want to change your study habits. If you find yourself reading a paragraph over and over again, try taking notes as you read, or read aloud. You can actually improve your powers of concentration by working on crossword, mathematical, or jigsaw puzzles. Figuring out short "whodunit" mysteries can be another fun way of flexing your concentration muscles.

> **What would you do**
>
> **if your grades started to slip after a loved one's death?**

If you're forgetful, use a notebook or organizer to write down your schedule, your assignments, or anything else you need to remember. Think of it as your back-up brain, and check it periodically. Ask an understanding friend to call and remind you when an important assignment is due.

I'm Just Not Me Anymore . . .

It is common to have trouble sleeping when you're grieving. You might very well be exhausted, but once your head hits the pillow you just can't stop thinking about death and dying. Getting enough sleep is important to your physical, mental, and emotional health—especially now. You might try drinking some warm milk with a dash of vanilla for flavor, or chamomile tea before going to bed. Avoid drinks with caffeine. Try taking a warm bath just before bedtime; practice emptying your mind of worries and fears, and imagine yourself lying on a warm beach or hiking your favorite woodland trail. There's a song that goes, "When the dog bites; When the bee stings; When I'm feeling sad; I simply remember my favorite things; And then I don't feel so bad." It may sound corny, but it helps.

You may find that food doesn't taste good anymore—you just don't want to eat. Or you can't resist all of the cake, cookies, chips and donuts that people brought to the house after the funeral. Remember that grieving is

Maintaining a healthy diet during the grieving process can be difficult. Some people have little or no appetite, while others indulge in obsessive eating as a way of comforting or distracting themselves.

hard work; your body needs high-quality fuel to get you through this period. Try to eat five small meals a day if you have a hard time with three big meals. Snack on popcorn or make yourself a fruit and yogurt smoothie. Chocolate actually contains a mood-boosting chemical. Don't be afraid to treat yourself to something you really like—just don't overdo it.

Are you more prone to accidents now that your loved one is gone? Researchers found that almost half of all adolescent boys who experienced the death of a parent in the past year had some kind of accident; about one third of these accidents required medical attention. The accident rate drops back to normal after that first difficult year. We are more likely to have accidents when we're grieving simply because we're not really paying attention to the world around us—we're consumed by our own thoughts and emotions. This is a time in your life when you should try to be a little more cautious.

Some teens deal with their grief by engaging in risky behaviors, reasoning, "Hey, life is short. I might as well live it up while I can!" You might be tempted to experiment with drugs or alcohol, steal a car for a joyride, or become sexually active. Drugs or alcohol might make you feel better for a very short time—as long as you are high. But when you come down off the high, you feel worse than ever. Drugs and alcohol cannot help you escape your grief; they'll leave you feeling worse than before. They may even kill you. When you're in pain, it can seem comforting to have someone hug you or hold you. But this is not the time to seek sexual intimacy: at best, you are likely to end up feeling ashamed and abandoned. At worst, you may add to your pain by becoming pregnant or contracting a sexually transmitted disease.

Grief Is Universal

We are not alone in experiencing grief when someone we love has died. Many animals also appear to express feelings of grief. In the book *When Elephants Weep: The Emotional Lives of Animals*, the authors tell the story of a male peregrine falcon whose mate disappeared, leaving him with five nestlings. He called for his mate for two days. On the third day, the male made an unfamiliar sound, "a cry like the screeching moan of a wounded animal, the cry of a creature in suffering . . . the sadness in the outcry was unmistakable," wrote the biologist who observed the falcon. "Having heard it, I will never doubt that an animal can suffer emotions that we humans think belong to our species alone."

Grief—in all of its faces—is not only normal, but necessary. Expressing your grief is one step in the work of **mourning** that will heal your wounded heart.

Honoring the Dead: Rituals, Funerals, and Memorial Services

Brooke's best friend, Lila, died of a brain tumor when both girls were thirteen years old. When Lila understood that she really was going to die, she took charge of things, just as she had always done. She researched donating her organs to science and convinced her parents to make the arrangements when she died. "I'll look down from heaven," Lila told Brooke, "and feel good because I'll see all those people walking around with parts of me in them."

Brooke woke up early the morning of Lila's funeral. She felt weak and jittery. Brooke had asked Lila's parents if she could read a poem at the funeral, one that the two friends had written together for a school assignment. Now she was having second thoughts. What if she cried? What would Lila's body look like? What if she did something wrong? The funeral service would be in a Methodist church. Brooke, who was Jewish, had never set foot inside a church. "Don't worry," her mother told her. "The important thing is that all of you are there to tell Lila goodbye, each in your own way."

Rituals surrounding death vary according to religion and culture. Funerals and other memorial occasions offer us a chance to say goodbye to a loved one and are an important step in accepting a loss.

At the church, Brooke joined the line of people walking slowly by Lila's casket. She was surprised to see that Lila looked fine—better, in fact, than she had in the final days before her death, when her face looked pinched and drawn. She touched Lila's hands, folded across her chest. They were cool and firm. Somehow, that made it easier to think of them lowering Lila's body into the ground—knew that her friend's spirit had really gone somewhere else. Reading the poem while trying to hold back tears was one of the hardest things Brooke had ever done, but afterwards she was glad she'd done it. She felt as though she had given her friend one last gift.

No matter what your religious background or ethnic heritage may be, the rituals that take place after death are an important first step in accepting the loss and saying goodbye to your loved one. Deciding what to do with the body is one of the first decisions the family must make after a loved one has died. If your loved one has chosen to be an organ donor, surgeons will remove one or more organs immediately after doctors determine that the brain has stopped working, and stitch the body back together. Knowing that their loved one's organs can save someone else's life may help ease the pain of families and friends.

Sometimes, doctors will ask the family for permission to perform an exam of the body, called an **autopsy**. The purpose of the autopsy is to answer questions about the person's illness or cause of death. A specially trained doctor, called a pathologist, examines the body, including internal organs and structures. After the autopsy, the pathologist closes any incisions made in the body, much as he or she would do following surgery.

> ## How would you feel
>
> **if your loved one chose to donate their organs, and that donation helped save someone's life?**

In many cases, the body undergoes a procedure called **embalming**, although some religious traditions forbid it. Embalming (the art of preserving bodies after death) probably began with the ancient Egyptians, who believed that this was a way of preparing the dead for their journey into the afterlife. Today, embalming involves washing and disinfecting the body to prevent the spread of disease, removing blood and other body fluids, and replacing them with chemicals that slow down decay and help color and soften the skin. Embalming helps preserve the body long enough for mourners to travel to the wake or funeral. Many psychologists believe that viewing the body of a loved one can help people accept their loss and move forward in the grieving process.

People of different cultures and religions have different ways of saying goodbye to their loved ones. You may feel

At a wake, family and friends gather to share their sorrow and offer sympathy to the family of the loved one. Expect to be hugged and comforted. There may even be laughter as you share stories from the good time's in your loved one's life.

anxious about the rituals surrounding the death of one you love, or be tempted to skip them altogether. But those who counsel the bereaved say that these rituals are an important part of the grieving process.

Sharing Sorrow

One common ritual is the visitation, or the wake. This is an informal gathering of friends and family before the funeral or memorial service, often at a church or funeral home. It is meant to give people a chance to share their sorrow and sympathy. Sometimes, but not always, mourners can view the body. You may want to contribute to this ritual by helping put together a photo album about the life of your loved one, or creating a collage that illustrates their love of a hobby or sport.

You may be surprised to find laughter along with the tears at a wake or visitation, as people trade stories about the person who died. Laughter is an important way of relieving tension; it is not necessarily a sign of disrespect. Expect to be hugged. If this makes you feel uncomfortable, remember that hugging or touching can convey feelings that people often cannot find the words to say.

Funerals and Memorial Services

A funeral or memorial service is more formal than a visitation or wake. A funeral is generally held within a few days after death, usually with the body present. A memorial service without the body present may be held later. Although the rituals can vary greatly from one religion to another, most services have these things in common: they honor the life of the person who has died, and they provide comfort to those who remain. Many people find that this is a time when they find particular comfort in their religious faith. Believing that the spirit of one who has died lives on, whether in an afterlife or through reincarnation, can give a great sense of comfort and hope. Even if you or your loved one did not believe in God or an afterlife, this can be an important time for you to celebrate your loved one's life and to keep his or her memory alive.

> ### What would you do
>
> **to make the funeral or memorial service of your loved one more meaningful to you?**

You may wish to help with the funeral or memorial service arrangements. Perhaps you would like to ask someone to sing your mother's favorite song at the funeral. You might want to tell a story about your friend, or ask to have someone else read a favorite poem or Bible passage. You could help select a favorite outfit for your loved one to be buried in.

After a funeral and burial, it is common for families to share a meal. It is an important time to exchange with others the memories you treasure.

Disposing of the Body

It is disturbing to think of disposing of the body of your loved one, but it is something that must be done. It helps to remember that the person you loved no longer inhabits that body. Nothing you can do hurts it.

In the United States, most people choose to bury their dead in a cemetery. The burial service usually takes place just after the funeral. You may have seen a funeral procession—a line of cars with their headlights on, headed for the cemetery. The minister, priest, or rabbi may say a few words and pray at the gravesite. In Jewish burials, family members throw or shovel handfuls of dirt into the grave to symbolize the body's return to dust and help them accept the finality of death. After the burial, family and friends often gather to share a meal or light snack. This, like the wake or visitation, is a time when people mix tears and laughter as they share their memories of the person who died.

Many people choose to cremate, or burn, the body of their loved one. In this country, the body is placed in a large oven, or **cremation** chamber, and heated to a very high temperature until all that is left are ashes and bone fragments. The funeral director gathers up the remains, places them into a container, and gives them to the family. Cremation is customary in some religious traditions, including Hinduism and Buddhism. Some people simply don't want to take up precious space on an increasingly crowded planet after they die, or would rather not spend the money on burial, which can be more expensive than cremation. Others choose cremation because their ashes can be scattered or buried in a place that they loved, such as over the ocean or in the mountains (although some states have restrictions about the scattering of remains).

What do you believe happens to our souls after we die?

Sitting Shiva

In the Jewish tradition, there is a period of mourning immediately following burial called shiva—usually seven days, but sometimes as few as three days. The grieving family is often said to be "sitting shiva," based on the custom of sitting low to the ground during this period. During shiva, the grieving family does not work or play, but stays at home, remembering their loved one and sharing in their grief. This is a time when friends and other family members can come and offer their condolences.

Informal Rituals

There many other informal rituals that may help you, your friends, and your family deal with the death of your loved one—not just immediately following the death, but for weeks, months, and even years to come. Write a message to your friend, tie it to a biodegradable balloon filled with helium, and let it go. If a teacher died of AIDS, think of asking classmates help you sew a square for an AIDS quilt; use the

> ### What would you do
>
> **in the weeks or months after the funeral or memorial service to commemorate your loved one?**

time you spend working together to talk about his or her life. A young woman whose father died of leukemia raised money for the Leukemia and Lymphoma Society by running in a marathon. On her shirt were the words, "For Dad." Training and running the marathon, she said, helped her let go of her father even as she kept his memory alive.

You may want to light a candle for your loved one on the anniversary of his death, or make his favorite chocolate cake and share it with your family on his birthday. These personal rituals can help to remind you that even though someone you cared about deeply has died, the love you had for each other lives on. It may seem impossible now, but over time, you may find that bringing your loved one's memory to life brings a smile to your face. As the poet Kahil Gibran wrote, "Remembrance is a form of meeting."

Nothing is the Same: How Families Change After Loss

■ Andy's father happened to be in the wrong place at the wrong time. He was waiting to pay for gas at a convenience store late one night when two young men panicked in a robbery attempt, killing him and the clerk. When Andy looked back on it, it seemed to him as though he had been transported to a parallel universe in that moment. Nothing was the same, yet all of the elements, except his dad, were in place.

Andy was still Andy—and yet now he was Andy, the boy whose father died. He still had a mother who loved him, two sisters and a brother, and a dog. Now his younger sister wanted the pacifier she had given up two years ago, and his once-mellow older sister was irritable and snappy. His older brother was no longer interested in skateboarding with Andy. All he wanted to do was listen to music, headphones on, in his room. Andy worried about his mother most of all. He often found her sitting at the kitchen table late at night, paying bills and scouring the want ads for better-paying jobs. She always looked tired, and she started

The loss of a loved one can profoundly change the way family members relate to each other. Family routines change, and you may find yourself taking on new responsibilities. A support group can help you accept these changes.

smoking again—a habit she'd quit last year.

When Andy's father died, he felt as though he lost not just a parent but a part of himself. Not only had he inherited his father's dark curly hair, but his quirky sense of humor and optimism as well. Now Andy felt as if both of those characteristics had died with his father. Andy had never dreamed that losing his father would change him and his family in so many ways.

When someone you love dies, it is as though someone threw a stone into a pond, sending ripples of loss wider and wider throughout your life. Everything changes.

The death of someone you loved will change you forever, but remember: you are still you. Over time, Andy will regain his quirky sense of humor and even his sense of optimism—they are as much a part of him as his black curly hair. Feeling different from everyone else is hard, though. This is why many teens find great comfort in joining a support group of others who have lost loved ones. It helps to be around other teens who can understand what you're talking about when you tell them how angry you are at your mother for dying—because they've been there, too. Often, support groups for grieving teens will simply arrange for an outing to an amusement park or a swimming party so that you can have some fun together.

Changes in Family Routines

Have you ever disturbed an ant nest? In an instant, the colony changes from an orderly unit to a collection of frenzied ants scrambling in many directions. While your family may not have been as orderly as an ant colony before your loved one died, you probably had a fairly predictable routine. Your sister takes out the trash, and you feed the dog. Granddad picks you up from school and takes you to your piano lesson. Your mom can be counted on to help with math homework, while you're better off asking your dad to proofread your English paper.

Can you describe how your family's routine changed since your loved one died?

Now, your family's routine is turned upside down: who will help you with your math homework? Who will take out the trash? But even ant colonies find a way to rebuild their nest, and your family will eventually work out a new routine, too. Perhaps you can take the bus to your piano lesson now, or you find that your older brother is pretty good at helping your with math homework. You may find yourself babysitting your little sister after school, or in

The loss of a loved one can create economic as well as emotional stress. There may be less money for movies, vacations, or groceries, and sometimes you may even have to move to a smaller house or apartment.

charge of the laundry. You had enough stress in your life before, what with homework, orchestra rehearsals, baseball practice—now this! Talk to your family about how all of you can balance your new responsibilities with time for yourselves. Remember all of those people who said at the funeral of your loved one, "If there's anything I can do, let me know." Don't be afraid to ask for help—it will ease the stress of an already difficult time.

But losing a family member means much more than losing a chauffeur or cook. When Andy's father died, his family was now faced with living off of one paycheck. A family that loses an important source of income may be forced to move to a smaller house with lower monthly payments. There may be less money for vacations, eating out, or going to the movies.

If both parents died, there will be an even bigger upheaval in your life. Not only are you dealing with two terrible losses, but you will almost surely have to move—perhaps to live with your grandparents, your aunt or uncle, an adult sibling, or a foster family. You may be faced with the challenge of enrolling in a new school, making new friends, or adapting to a new family—even as you're grieving for your parents. Maintaining connections with your old life as you adapt to your new one will help. Try to stay in touch with your friends. Meet them for a movie or lunch, if your new home is close enough. Talk to your guardians about using the telephone, e-mail or instant messaging to stay in touch if you've moved far away from your friends. Keep things that remind you of your parents and your old home, such as pictures, a favorite quilt, or the clock that chimed on the mantel.

In some families, the father plays the role of coach— teaching you how to dance, whistle, or swing a tennis racket while the mother serves as a kind of anchor—

Do you know

a caring adult who could spend some time with you if your parent or guardian died?

bandaging your scraped knees or holding you when you cry about not getting a role in the school play. If you are a boy whose father has died, or a girl who lost her mother, you may wonder who you can talk to about all of the changes going on with your body. Who will teach you to shave? Who can you talk to about menstruation?

Of course no one can ever replace a parent, but it may help to find an older relative or friend of the family who can play tennis with you like your dad used to do, or who will take you out for ice cream and listen to your worries. Big Brothers and Big Sisters of America is a wonderful organization that matches up kids and teens, most of them from single parent homes, with adult volunteers who are willing to play, give advice, or just listen.

Losing a sibling can be a great shock. Young people aren't supposed to die! If you lost a younger sibling, you may feel that you have been cheated out of the chance to teach her important skills such as riding a bike or putting a worm on a fishing hook. Even though your younger brother or sister could be bratty, you lost someone who looked up to you. If an older sibling died, you lost a role model, the one who stood up for you when kids at school picked on you.

Teens sometimes feel as though it is their duty to fill the shoes their older brother or sister left empty after death. If your brother was a football star, you might feel an urge to try out for the football team—even though you much preferred playing in the marching band. It is common to remember a dead sibling as superhuman, forgetting their shortcomings while playing up their strengths. You might remember the fact that your sister had a remarkable talent for making people laugh, while forgetting that she often used her sharp sense of humor to belittle you. Remember that you are one of a kind, just as your sibling was a unique person. Think about what makes *you* happy. Work on developing your skills in things *you* are good at.

Being a part of a family that has lost a loved one is never easy. Each family member mourns loss in his or her own way. It is very common for children to behave in ways that they outgrew months or years ago: younger children who are potty trained may start having frequent

You may feel the need to step into the role of a loved one who has died—taking up the hobbies or activities that person left unfinished. Remember that you are an individual—seek out the things that bring *you* joy.

"accidents," for example. Other children may become wild and out of control; some may withdraw from the rest of the family.

Your parent may even be so consumed by grief through the loss of a family member that he or she has a hard time helping you with your emotional needs. You may feel that all of your mother's energy is focused on grieving for your brother, with nothing left for you. It may be hard for you to cry around your mother if you feel that it would make her feel too bad. Find a caring relative or friend who will listen to you. If you are concerned about the well-being of one of your parents, tell a relative or friend. He or she may be able to get help for your parents. If you lost a sibling, you may feel that your parents will smother you with their over-protectiveness. Talk to them about their fears and try to work out a plan that will allow you to have some freedom while reassuring them about your safety.

What would you do

if you were not getting the emotional support you need from other family members?

It Wasn't Supposed to be Like This: Special Circumstances

■ Mr. Nolan was one of the best-loved teachers in school. He taught math with such enthusiasm that his students—even those who thought they hated math—willingly put in extra hours to solve the clever puzzles he assigned to them. Students knew that they could confide in Mr. Nolan when they needed to talk about their problems, and was a frequent chaperone at school dances. He kept his private life private, however. All anyone knew was that he wasn't married.

Over the course of the school year, Diane and her friends noticed that Mr. Nolan seemed to be losing weight. He stopped chaperoning their dances, and seemed less energetic than usual. He began to joke about "retiring" so that he could enjoy his old age, even though he was only 40 years old. One day, about a month before summer break, a substitute came in to teach Mr. Nolan's class, telling the students that their teacher was too ill to finish out the school year. No one could tell the students what was wrong with Mr. Nolan.

Mr. Nolan died that summer. When they returned to school

that fall, the principal held a special assembly and told the students that Mr. Nolan had died of complications of AIDS. He had asked the principal not to tell the children about his illness until after he died, fearing that he would be harassed or forced to resign. Diane was stunned. AIDS didn't happen here, not in this small southern town.

The students were strangely quiet following the assembly. No one knew what to say. The new math teacher, Ms. Barker, began class by saying, "Before I start teaching you math, I want to talk about the elephant in this room. What I mean is that there's something great big going on here, but no one wants to talk about it. We all want to ignore it and hope it goes away, but it won't. I think that what Mr. Nolan would have wanted us to lift the shame from AIDS."

Losing a loved one is never easy, but some deaths are especially upsetting or hard to talk about. AIDS is one of them. So is death by suicide, alcohol abuse, or a drug overdose. These are sometimes called **"stigmatic deaths,"** meaning that they were the result of an illness or lifestyle that many people in our society do not approve of. (The Greek word "stigma" means mark, or tattoo.)

Other deaths occur under such violent or frightening circumstances that they leave the survivors with emotional wounds that heal very slowly. Many people who lost loved ones in the bombing of the federal building in Oklahoma City in 1995 or in the September 11th attack on the World Trade Center and the Pentagon in 2001, develop long-lasting symptoms called **post-traumatic stress disorder**, or PTSD.

AIDS

If someone you love has died of AIDS, or Acquired Immune Deficiency Syndrome, your grief may be mixed with feelings of humiliation or disgrace. Sadly, our culture

Some of the circumstances surrounding a death are especially hard to talk about. AIDS is one example. Remember that AIDS is caused by a virus, not a lifestyle. Nobody deserves to die of an AIDS-related death.

is often quick to pass judgment on people who do not fit into the popular definition of "normal." But the simple truth is, AIDS is not a disease of gay men or intravenous drug users; it is a disease caused by a virus transmitted by bodily

fluids. The HIV virus that causes AIDS can infect men and women of any sexual orienta-
tion. It can infect children and adolescents as well as adults. It does not discrimi-
nate between rich and poor, or between black and white.

How would you feel

if a family member or friend told you they had HIV/AIDS?

In short, it infects both genders, all races and cultural backgrounds, and people of all ages.

Unfortunately, at least half of all new HIV infections in the U.S. are among people under the age of 25; most of them become infected through unprotected sex. In people between the ages of 13 and 19, 64% of the new HIV infections are reported in young women; over half are African American.

If it was your brother who died of AIDS, remember that he was your brother, no matter what. Don't let prejudices get in the way of your grief. Educate your-self about the disease that cut short the life of your loved one. The best defense against HIV infection is information. If you and your family feel comfortable talking about HIV/AIDS, you could create a mean-ingful memorial to your loved one by helping educate others about the disease and its prevention. Many communities have HIV/AIDS support groups that can help you deal with the death of your loved one in a non-judgmental way.

Suicide

Suicide is the eighth leading cause of death nationwide, and the third leading cause of death among young people age 15-24. If someone you loved died by suicide, you are likely to be hit by a barrage of reactions: shock, guilt, anger, and depression. You may even feel relieved if you've

It is important not to let societal prejudices get in the way of your grief. Coping with an AIDS-related loss should involve more communication, not less. There may be organizations in your community that can help.

witnessed your loved one's long decline into self-destructive behavior and mental anguish. You are frustrated because you can't make sense out of such a senseless act. The most important thing to understand is this: it was not your fault.

There is a saying: "Suicide is not chosen; it happens when pain exceeds resources for coping with pain." If your best friend took her life, it wasn't because she was a bad or weak person; she was carrying more pain than she could deal with at the time. There are many types of pain that can lead to suicide, but the most common are clinical depression and other mental illnesses. The trouble with suicide as a method for escaping pain is

What would you do

if a friend talked to you about ending his or her life?

that there are better ways of dealing with the pain. Most situations change or get better with time, but suicide is forever.

Even though people are often uncomfortable talking about suicide, you need to talk about your feelings of loss and pain. Taking the initiative to talk about your loved one and the suicide will help you and others. You may find it easiest to talk with other suicide survivors. The American Foundation for Suicide Prevention, listed in the Further Reading section of this book, can provide you with a directory of support groups for suicide survivors.

When a teen dies by suicide, occasionally one or more "copycat" suicides will follow. These suicide outbreaks may be triggered by a misplaced sense of loyalty to a dead friend, deep depression, or a sense that suicide is somehow "romantic," like the two lovers in *Romeo and Juliet*. If you have any of these feelings, please remember how much your friend's death hurt you and his family. Would you want to do that to the people who love you?

Violence and Disasters

If your loved one died a violent death or in a natural or man-made disaster, you are recovering from a very painful and shocking experience. If you witnessed the

Sudden and violent losses, like those that occur through murder, terrorism, or natural disasters can be especially hard to accept. Vigils or other services can help us process the overwhelming emotions that result from such losses.

killing, or if you were the one to discover your loved one's body, your shock is likely to be even greater. Our country has been shaken by several major acts of violence in recent years—the 2001 terrorist attacks on the World Trade Center and the Pentagon; the shootings at Columbine High School in Littleton, Colorado in 1999; and the bombing of the Alfred P. Murrah Federal Building in Oklahoma City, to name just a few. In 1999,

52 people lost their lives when Hurricane Floyd swept through North Carolina; many more were injured or lost their homes. If you are a survivor, you may wonder whether your emotional wounds will ever heal. They can, but it will take time and loving support.

The stress of losing a loved one to a man-made or natural disaster can lead to emotional problems that show up weeks, or even months later. National tragedies, such as the terrorist attacks on the World Trade Center and the Pentagon, can cause deep emotional wounds, even in people who were not in any way connected to the event. One-third of the survivors of the Oklahoma City bombing developed post-traumatic stress disorder (PTSD), a condition often seen in veterans of the Vietnam War. Some of the most common symptoms of PTSD are flashbacks, hallucinations, and frequent thoughts about the traumatic event, nightmares, intense anxiety, or angry outbursts. You feel as though the event is happening all over again, like a videotape that plays over and over again in your brain. At other times, you try to avoid any thoughts or feelings that remind you of this tragedy. You make yourself numb, unable to feel sadness or happiness. You may not even recall important events surrounding the death of your loved one. Many people who have PTSD say that they feel jumpy and restless; they have trouble sleeping and concentrating.

> **How did you feel** when you heard about the September 11th attacks—even if you didn't know any of the victims?

If these feelings last for more than a week, it is important that you talk to an adult who can arrange for you to see a therapist to help you heal this deep emotional wound. It is unlikely to go away by itself. Don't forget to take care of yourself: take a walk in a park or spend some quiet time in your church, synagogue, or mosque. Spend time with your friends and family, and allow yourself to talk about your feelings.

The Elephant in the Room

The death of a loved one can be so devastating that it seems take over your whole life, leaving very little room for you to think about anything but the person you lost. No matter how hard you try, the reality of the death cannot be avoided. But as Terry Kettering makes clear in the following poem, you should not try to avoid this reality. It is through talking about the death of your loved one that you will begin to heal, and replace your grief with happy memories of your loved one's life.

The Elephant in the Room

There's an elephant in the room.

It is large and squatting, so it is hard to get around it.

Yet we squeeze by with, "How are you" and "I'm fine."

And a thousand other forms of trivial chatter.

We talk about the weather.

We talk about work.

We talk about everything—except the elephant in the room.

There's an elephant in the room.

We all know it is there.

We are thinking about the elephant as we talk together.

It is constantly on our minds.

For you see, it is a very big elephant.

It has hurt us all.

But we do not talk about the elephant in the room.

Oh please say her name.

Oh please say "Barbara" again.

Oh please, let's talk about the elephant in the room.

For if we talk about her death,

Perhaps we can talk about her life?

Can I say "Barbara" to you and not have you look away?

For if I cannot, then you are leaving Me

Alone . . .

In a room . . .

With an elephant.

(Bereavement Publishers, Inc.)

Adjusting to
a New Life

■ Patrick's fondest memories of his mother, Beth, were of her covered with dirt and sweat after an afternoon's work in the garden. "Let's have a glass of lemonade," she would suggest, "I'm beat." Together they would sit on the garden bench, drinking the puckery lemonade and talking about everything from the medicinal properties of plants to Patrick's ambition to be a drummer. Even after she got too sick to work in the garden, this was where the two of them came when they wanted to talk.

And so it was that one year after his mother died of breast cancer, Patrick asked his father if he could plant a tree in his mother's memory. "I don't feel like I'm close to her when we visit her grave at the cemetery," he explained to his father. "It's like a golf course all scattered with tombstones—not at all like her garden." His father agreed, and together they went to a nursery and picked out a flowering crabapple tree, one that would bloom in the spring and provide food for the birds in the winter. Patrick and his father worked together to dig a deep hole for the young tree. As they dug, they

Adjusting to life after a loss can be difficult. So many things remind us of that person and the important role they filled for us.

talked about Beth's dying, and all that they had been through together in the months that followed her death.

They gently lowered the tree into the hole and shoveled dirt around the roots as they watered it. Patrick thought about how it would grow over the years, giving food and shelter to birds and squirrels, and felt a bittersweet kind of happiness. When they finished, Patrick and his father drank ice-cold lemonade on the bench near their new tree. He would always miss his mother, and he knew that his father would, too. But they made it through this first year, day by day, and they would make it through the years to come.

Even as you make progress in recovering from your loss, you will encounter some rough spots in which you find yourself grieving all over again. Holidays and birthdays can be difficult times, especially in the first year or two following the death of a loved one.

Making it Through Holidays, Anniversaries, and Birthdays

From October 31 to January 2, you are constantly reminded that people are preparing to celebrate and spend time with people they love. Everyone else seems to be so happy! The last thing you feel like doing is giving thanks or seeking joy. Or you may really be looking forward to all of the food, gifts, and parties that the holidays usually bring—and then wonder if it's okay to have fun now. Remember that enjoying yourself is not disrespectful to your loved one. Laughter can help heal your wounds. At the same time, don't be afraid to cry, even while everyone around you seems to be having a good time. Your feelings are your own.

There are things you can do to make the holidays easier for you and your family. This is an especially important time to talk with your friends and family about what you would like to do this holiday season. You and your family might find comfort in observing your family and religious rituals—going to Midnight Mass on Christmas Eve, making latkes during Chanukah, or lighting the Kwanzaa candles. Other families find that a change of scenery or establishing new traditions make the holidays easier. If you enjoy making Christmas cookies, consider taking them to a homeless shelter this year. Perhaps your family would prefer eating at a Chinese restaurant on Thanksgiving.

How would you change your holiday rituals, if at all, after the death of a loved one?

Think of ways that you can remember your loved one in holiday rituals. Ask friends and family to write something they remember about your loved one on cards and put them

Holidays, anniversaries, and birthdays can be particularly challenging times when we are grieving. Sharing your holiday plans with friends and family is one step toward recovery. You may even be able to memorialize your loved one through holiday rituals.

in his Christmas stocking so that you and your family can read them together. As you light the Chanukah or Kwanzaa candles, light a separate one for your loved one and say a prayer for her.

There will be many special occasions that remind you of how much you miss your loved one. Don't pretend that Mother's Day doesn't matter because your mother has died. You may want to write her a long letter each year and send it up in a biodegradable helium balloon. If your father has died, you may wish to send a thank-you card on Father's Day to an uncle or mentor who listened when you needed to talk. If your sister loved to read, donate a book to the library in her memory.

Just as the date September 11, 2001 has taken on a new meaning for most people in this country, the date that your loved one died now holds a special significance to you. In the Jewish faith, there is often a ceremony one year after the death in which friends and family gather to unveil the tombstone. Whatever your religious background, the anniversary of your loved one's death may bring a tidal wave of emotions. Take the time to remember her in a way that holds meaning for you: plant a tree in her memory, visit his grave, or light a candle.

Especially if you have lost a parent or sibling, you will find yourself reminded of your loss as you mature and mark special milestones in your life—your bat or bar mitzvah, confirmation, your high school graduation, or your wedding. These events call for a celebration, but they may very well trigger fresh feelings of grief as well. You may find yourself grieving years after your initial loss when you move from your family home. Talk to your friends and family about the way you're feeling. You may find that they are grieving all over again, as well.

Loving Again

If your mother or father died, there is a possibility that your remaining parent might want to date again or even remarry—not right away, but after the pain has subsided and your mom or dad feels stronger and ready to go on with life. This is a good sign: it means that your parent is healing from a horrible blow. Even so, the thought of another adult intruding on your family circle may frighten or upset you.

Does this mean that your dad has already forgotten your mother? Or that some strange man will come into your life try to take the place of your father? Have a heart-to-heart talk with your mom or dad. Let him or her know how you're feeling.

What would you do

if you didn't like the woman your father was dating after the death of your mother?

What if you hate your mom's date? You should be allowed to express your opinions to your mom, but remember that the rules of common courtesy apply. If you can't stand the thought of your dad's date sitting in your mom's favorite chair, let him know—politely. You may also feel uncomfortable with the idea of you parent dating again because you were just getting used to things the way they were. Now, things are changing all over again.

As hard as it may be for you to accept, it is normal and healthy for a parent to want to develop a close relationship with another person after losing a spouse. It is not disloyal to love again after losing a husband, wife, or partner. Nor is it disloyal for you to like the person your father is dating.

In the same vein, if your best friend died, it is not a sign of disloyalty to forge new friendships. If the guy you'd been dating was killed in a car wreck, it is okay to date again, but be careful that you don't let your grief lead you into a sexually intimate situation that you are not ready to handle.

Life Goes On

Some days you will feel as though you are climbing Mount Everest: you move forward five feet, and then fall back two. Mourning the loss of someone you love can be

Mourning a loss can seem like a hard climb. But some days will be better than others, and you may be surprised by your own recovery. As your acceptance of your new life grows, remember to share your feelings with those around you.

a long, difficult climb. Will you ever reach the peak—or will you know it if you do? You will always miss your loved one, but mountain climbers say that when they reach the top of the mountain, they see the world from a different perspective.

Many people learn that grief forces them to look more closely at their beliefs and values. Is there a God? Why are we here? What does it mean to live a good life? Things we took for granted—our family and friends, the place we call home and the food we eat—become precious. The things we used to think were important now seem trivial.

Sure, it would be nice to have the sneakers everyone else is wearing—but it's no longer essential. There is a song by The Pretenders that ends with the words, "What's important in this life? Ask the man who's lost his wife."

You may not even realize that you are recovering from your loss until you wake up one day and find yourself eagerly looking forward to the day ahead. Thinking of your loved one, wearing a piece of her jewelry, or hearing his favorite song on the radio no longer brings you pain, but comfort. You have come to accept things as they are, not as you wish they would be. You can have fun without feeling guilty.

Now that you have experienced a great loss, your life will never be the same. But for most teens, the pain of grief lessens, slowly but surely. They are able to let go of their loss and get on with living life, even as they cherish the memory of the one they loved. Helen Keller wrote, "What we have once enjoyed and deeply loved we can never lose, for all that we loved deeply becomes a part of us."

Glossary

Autopsy – an examination of the body of a person who has died, for the purpose of determining the cause of death.

Cremation – the process of burning a human corpse, reducing it to ashes and bone fragments.

Depression – a mood or emotional state marked by sadness, inactivity, and a reduced ability to enjoy life.

Embalming – the practice of disinfecting and temporarily preserving a corpse.

Grief – a set of reactions when someone has experienced an important loss. Grief can take many different forms: strong emotions, bodily sensations, thought patterns and dreams, and behaviors.

Mourning – the ways in which we learn to live with and find meaning in our loss.

Post-traumatic stress disorder – an anxiety disorder that causes the sufferer to relive a trauma, to avoid situations similar to that trauma, and to be anxious and expectant of future traumatic events.

Rituals – ceremonial acts that mark important events in our lives. Rituals discussed in this book include funerals, memorial services, and sitting shiva.

Stigmatic death – a death that is especially hard to talk about or deal with because it was the result of what some people in our society believe to be unacceptable behavior.

Stress – anything that disturbs our normal functioning. Stress can be either positive (falling in love) or negative (losing a parent). Either way, it can have important effects on our minds and bodies.

Further Reading

Books—Nonfiction:

Fitzgerald, Helen. *The Grieving Teen: A Guide for Teenagers and Their Friends.* New York: Fireside, 2000.

Fry, Virginia Lynn. *Part of Me Died, Too: Stories of Creative Survival Among Bereaved Children and Teenagers.* New York: Dutton Children's Books, 1995.

Gootman, Marilyn E. *When a Friend Dies: A Book for Teens About Grieving and Healing.* Minneapolis: Free Spirit Publishing, Inc., 1994.

Grollman, Earl A. *Straight Talk About Death for Teenagers: How to Cope With Losing Someone You Love.* Boston: Beacon Press, 1993.

Krementz, Jill. *How it Feels When a Parent Dies.* New York: Alfred A. Knopf, 1981.

Wolfelt, Alan. *Healing Your Grieving Heart for Teens: 100 Practical Ideas.* Fort Collins, CO: Companion Press, 2001.

Books—Fiction:

Blume, Judy. *Tiger Eyes.* Scarsdale, NY: Bradbury Press, 1987.

Greene, Constance C. *Beat the Turtle Drum.* New York: Viking Press, 1976.

Paterson, Katherine. *Bridge to Terabithia.* New York: Harper and Row, 1979.

Web sites:

A Place to Grieve. *http://www.newhope-grief.org/teengrief/*

American Foundation for Suicide Prevention: *http://www.afsp.org/*

Barr-Harris Children's Grief Center. *http://www.barrharris.org/*

Julie's Place: A Website for Bereaved Siblings. *http://www.juliesplace.com/*

The Dougy Center for Grieving Children. *http://www.dougy.org/*

Rainbows. *http://www.rainbows.org/*

National Funeral Director's Association. *http://www.nfda.org/resources/caregiving/*

Big Brothers Big Sisters of America: *http://www.bbbsa.org*

Index

Index

About the Author

Sara L. Latta is a writer living in Illinois. She has written extensively about health and medicine, including two young adult books on allergies and food poisoning. When she is not writing, she enjoys spending time with her family, running, reading, and gardening.

About the Editor

Marvin Rosen is a licensed clinical psychologist who practices in Media, Pennsylvania. He received his doctorate degree from the University of Pennsylvania in 1961. Since 1963, he has worked with intellectually and emotionally challenged people at Elwyn, Inc. in Pennsylvania, with clinical, administrative, research, and training responsibilities. He also conducts a private practice of psychology. Dr. Rosen has taught psychology at the University of Pennsylvania, Bryn Mawr College, and West Chester University. He has written or edited seven book and numerous professional articles in the areas of psychology, rehabilitation, emotional disturbance, and mental retardation.